T0199133

PENTAWHADDA!

Lynn Calvin Plater

WestBow Press books may be ordered through booksellers or by contacting:

WestBow Press
A Division of Thomas Nelson & Zondervan
1663 Liberty Drive
Bloomington, IN 47403
www.westbowpress.com
844-714-3454

ISBN: 978-1-6642-7276-7 (sc)
ISBN: 978-1-6642-7277-4 (e)

Library of Congress Control Number: 2022913125

Print information available on the last page.

WestBow Press rev. date: 08/05/2022

WESTBOW
PRESS®
A DIVISION OF THOMAS NELSON
& ZONDERVAN

This book is dedicated to my cousin Iona Hutton, a professional teacher who taught me through fun games.

"Good morning, class!" says Mrs. Prazer.

"Good morning, Mrs. Prazer!" says the class.

"Today is the last Friday of the month, a half of a day of school, and you know what that means," says Mrs. Prazer.

"Yes, it's Special Guest Friday—no classwork for the day and no homework for the weekend!" yells one person in the class.

"That's correct. Today we are going to have a guest teacher for our special guest. Her name is Mrs. Bibel, and she is going to teach us about some books of the Bible," says Mrs. Prazer.

The class cheers. "Yay! Yay! Yay!"

Mrs. Prazer says, "I know you are excited, but I need you to listen so we can learn. Let's get in our listening position."

"Ready!" says the class.

"Put your right hand in your imaginary right pocket, pull out your right listening ear, and hold it in the air. Shake it out to get the dust bunnies off. Place it over your right ear. Adjust it to make sure it fits. When your right listening ear is on, place your right hand on the desk."

Mrs. Prazer waits while the children adjust their right listening ears, observing to see whether any of the children need help. When she sees that all the children have their right hands on their desks, she says, "Good job, class! Now, put your left hand in your imaginary left pocket, pull out your left listening ear, and hold it in the air. Shake it out to get the dust bunnies off. Place it over your left ear. Adjust it to make sure it fits. When your left listening ear is on, place your left hand on the desk."

Again, Mrs. Prazer waits while the children adjust their left listening ears, observing to see whether any of the children need help. When she sees that all the children have their left hands on their desks, she says, "Wonderful job, class! From now until it is time to go home, Mrs. Bibel will be teaching us about some books of the Bible. Let's welcome Mrs. Bibel with a clap!" The class claps as Mrs. Bibel comes to the front of the class.

"Good morning, class!" says Mrs. Bibel with a great big smile. "Are you ready to learn about some books of the Bible?"

The class leans into their desks and says, "Good morning, Mrs. Bibel! We are ready!"

"All right!" says Mrs. Bibel. "Raise your right hand, and wiggle your fingers."

The children in the class raise their right hands and wiggle their fingers. Mrs. Bibel does this with them.

"Starting with our thumbs touching our pinky fingers, we are going to count from one to five. Let's begin."

Mrs. Bibel and the class count together. "One, two, three, four, five. Great job!" says Mrs. Bibel. "We are going to learn the first five books of the Bible, but first, I have to tell you a story. Do you like stories, class?"

"Oh, yes," says the class.

"Super!" says Mrs. Bibel.

"One day, long ago, there was a man named Moses. Can you say Moses, class?"

"Moses," says the class.

"He listened to what God told him and wrote it down in these five books so that children today can read it and know what God did and said."

"Ooooooooohhhh," says the class.

"Now these five books have a special name."

"What is it?" yelled the class, listening intently.

"It's a big word," says Mrs. Bibel, gaining the interest of the class.

"Tell us, please, please, please," says the class excitedly.

Pent

Penta

Pentateuch

7

"OK, but I'll write it first. Then I'll sound it out, and I'll tell you what it means." Mrs. Bibel writes PENTATEUCH on the board. She places her right hand over the last six letters on the board and says, "Pent." She removes her right hand from the letter *A* and says, "Ah." Then she removes her right hand from the rest of the word and says, "Tuke," with a sneeze-like motion. Mrs. Bibel then pronounces the entire word: Pentateuch.

The class says, "Pentawhadda?"

Mrs. Bibel laughs and repeats the word: "Pentateuch! Now, repeat after me. Ready, begin. Pent!"

"Pent," says the class.

"Ah," says Mrs. Bibel.

"Ah," says the class.

"Tuke," says Mrs. Bibel with a sneeze-like motion.

"Tuke," says the class with a sneeze-like motion.

"Pentateuch," says Mrs. Bibel,

"Pentateuch," says the class.

"Excellent!" says Mrs. Bibel.

The students cheer, clap, and give each other high-fives.

Mrs. Bibel says, "OK, settle down; I promised to tell you what it means."

"Oh, yeah," says the class.

Mrs. Bibel says, "*Penta* means five, and *teuch* means books. When you put the two parts together, they equal five books of the Bible. They are at the beginning of the Bible, so they are called the first five books of the Bible. They are Genesis, Exodus, Leviticus, Numbers, and Deuteronomy.

5 + GENESIS EXODUS LEVITICUS NUMBERS DEUTERONOMY = PENTATEUCH

Genesis means 'in the beginning.' Exodus means 'the road out,' or what we call the exit. Leviticus means 'someone who belongs to the Levites.' Levites were people that God chose to be priests, and He gave them rules, or what we call laws, about what to do. This book is called the first law. Numbers means 'the numbering or counting,' and Deuteronomy means 'the second law.' That's the end of the story. Raise your hand again; we are going to count, starting with your pinky finger touching your thumb. Now, repeat after me. One, Genesis."

The class says, "One, Genesis."

"Good!" says Mrs. Bibel. "Two, Exodus." Mrs. Bibel touches her ring finger to her thumb.

"Two, Exodus," says the class as they touch their ring fingers to their thumbs.

"Great!" says Mrs. Bibel. "Three, Leviticus." Mrs. Bibel touches her middle finger to her thumb.

"Three, Leviticus," says the class as they touch their middle fingers to their thumbs.

"Wonderful!" says Mrs. Bibel. "Four, Numbers." Mrs. Bibel touches her index finger to her thumb.

"Four, Numbers," says the children as they touch their index fingers to their thumbs.

"Super!" says Mrs. Bibel. "Five, Deu-te-ron-o-my." Mrs. Bibel speaks slowly so the children can repeat after her as she opens her hand wide.

"Five, Deu-te-ron-o-my," says the class slowly, like Mrs. Bibel said it, as they open their hands wide.

"Excellent!" says Mrs. Bibel. "That is a hard word to pronounce. Since it's almost time to go home, let's play a quick game to help us remember these names. Ready to play?" asks Mrs. Bibel,

"Yes!" shouts the class.

"OK," says Mrs. Bibel. "Turn to the person on your right and say, 'Gene has a sis.'"

The children in the class turn to the people on their right and say, "Gene has a sis."

"Good!" says Mrs. Bibel. "Now, turn to the person on your left and say, 'Genesis!'"

The children in the class turn to the people on their left and say, "Genesis!"

"While you are turned to the person on your left, say, 'Oh dear, let us exit.'"

The children in the class say to the people on their left, "Oh dear, let us exit."

"Good job!" says Mrs. Bibel. "Now, turn back to the person on your right and say, 'Exodus.'"

The children in the class turn back to the people on their right and say, "Exodus."

"Now push your chair back from your desk and stand up in front of your chair. Place your right hand over your heart, as if you are saying the Pledge of Allegiance, and say, 'Leave it inside of us.'"

The children do as Mrs. Bibel says.

"Now keep your hand on your heart and say, 'Leviticus.'"

The class says, "Leviticus."

"Great job!" says Mrs. Bibel.

14

"Take your right hand away from your heart and hold it in the air. Then put your left hand in the air and count all your fingers together."

The class counts from one to ten.

"Now say, 'Numbers,'" says Mrs. Bibel.

"Numbers," shouts the class.

"Wonderful job, class! OK, this is the last one," says Mrs. Bibel. "High-five the person on your right and say, 'Do to Ron or me.'"

The children in the class high-five the people on their right and say, "Do to Ron or me."

"Now high-five the person on your left and say, 'Deuteronomy,'" says Mrs. Bibel.

The children in the class high-five the people on their left and say, "Deuteronomy."

"Excellent work, class! Give yourselves a hand."

The class claps.

Mrs. Bibel says, "That's it for the day. I'll see you next time!" Mrs. Bibel exchanges seats with Mrs. Prazer.

Mrs. Prazer asks the class, "Did you have fun learning those books of the Bible?"

The class cheers, whistles, claps, and roars, "Yeah, that was fun!"

Mrs. Prazer agrees. "It was fun, wasn't it? Now, before we leave, I need you to take your listening ears off, put them back in your imaginary pockets, take them home, wash them out, and bring them back Monday. Let's gather our books and belongings and line up at the door."

The children gather their books and belongings and line up at the door. They walk in a double line to their lockers to get their coats, and then they go home excited and ready to share what they learned in school today with family, friends, and others.

The End

Thank You For An Amazing Day!

Song: Pentawhadda

(Chorus)

Pentawhadda,

Pentawhodda,

Pentawhadda,

The Pentateuch.

(Repeat)

I'm talking about Genesis and Exodus,

Leviticus and Numbers too.

Deuteronomy is the last book in the Penta, the Pentateuch.

(Repeat chorus)

Genesis—the beginning.

Exodus—the exit.

Leviticus is the first law in the Penta, the Pentateuch.

Then there's Numbers—the counting—

And Deuteronomy, the second law.

These are the five books in the Penta—

The Penta—the Pentateuch

(Repeat the chorus three times and fade toward the end)

Contact Information

CYLS-KIDS, LLC
Website: www.mycylskids.com
E-mail: cyls.kids@mycylskids.com

For in-person or on-line author readings, please complete
the Inquiry Form on the Contact page of the website.

Printed in the United States
by Baker & Taylor Publisher Services